dwarf &
mini rabbits

understanding and
caring for your pet

Written by
Dr Anne McBride BSc PhD Cert.Cons FRSA

dwarf &
mini rabbits

understanding and
caring for your pet

Written by
Dr Anne McBride BSc PhD Cert.Cons FRSA

Magnet & Steel Ltd

www.magnetsteel.com

Printed and bound in South Korea.

ISBN: 978-1-907337-02-4
ISBN: 1-907337-02-4

|Contents

Perfect pets

Rabbits make great pets and, while the larger varieties are perhaps more suitable for children, dwarf and mini rabbits are delicate and attractive to keep. If treated gently they are friendly and enjoy being stroked.

Throughout this book the term 'Dwarf rabbits' will include Mini rabbits, unless specifically stated otherwise.

Dwarf rabbits can live for 10 years, and sometimes longer. They are not expensive to buy. Once you have bought your initial equipment they are relatively inexpensive to feed and house, compared to a cat or dog.

However, be aware that appropriate accommodation may be costly, while feed and veterinary fees, such as for vaccinations and neutering, must be factored into your decision to obtain rabbits, of any size, as pets.

In addition, some dwarf rabbits are particularly susceptible to dental problems, which can prove to be very expensive as they will require lifelong treatment.

You may want to take out pet insurance to cover veterinary fees.

Ideally you should have two dwarf rabbits, to provide companionship for each other, and added warmth if they live outside. Dwarf rabbits are not as hardy as their larger relatives and thus are not as easy to keep outside if the weather is very cold. The outside accommodation should comprise of a hutch and attached run. The hutch must be kept warm and draught free, and must be sheltered from rain and wind. Like all rabbits, dwarf rabbits can also overheat easily and must be kept in the shade in the summer.

Dwarf rabbits can be kept as house rabbits. They can live inside, in a suitably-sized cage and attached exercise area, and can spend some time roaming free in other safe areas of the house.

Dwarf rabbits are most active in the early morning and the evening. Some small animals, such as hamsters, are active at night.

Some people are allergic to the fur of animals and may suffer health problems if a pet is kept in the house. Your doctor can test for this and, if you have a problem, you may still keep your rabbits outside in a hutch with a run attached and enjoy watching them.

Special requirements

Dwarf rabbits are extremely appealing, with their large eyes, small ears, rounded heads and tiny bodies. But, like all animals, they have their own special requirements which you need to know about before buying your first dwarf rabbits. This is important so you can have a good relationship with your pets, and they can live long, healthy and happy lives.

- You will need to handle your dwarf rabbits gently as they are easily frightened, especially when picked up. They also have small, fragile bones. This is why they are not particularly suitable pets for children.

- You need to give your dwarf rabbits the right food to stay fit and healthy. All rabbits have a special requirement for high fibre food.

- You will need to frequently clean out the dwarf rabbits' home.

- You need to provide a large, safe area where your dwarf rabbits can exercise every day outside their hutch or cage.

- You will need to make arrangements for someone to look after your dwarf rabbits if you go away on holiday.

You will need to register your dwarf rabbits with a veterinary practice.

They will need to have their teeth checked by a vet every few weeks. In addition, they require vaccinating against Myxomatosis twice a year, and annually for VHD (see page 116). These illnesses can kill dwarf rabbits, even if they are kept indoors.

Checks you can do yourself on a weekly basis include coat, weight, teeth and nails.

What is a dwarf rabbit?

Wild Ancestors

The wild ancestors of all our pet rabbits originally came from Spain and Portugal. Pet rabbits, including dwarf rabbits, share the same basic behaviours and needs as their wild cousins. So in order to understand your dwarf rabbits better it is useful to know how their wild cousins live.

Fossil remains of rabbits date back over 4,000 years. Known as the European rabbit, it is one of the most successful of all small animals and is famous for being able to quickly populate an area. This is because their needs are simple. So long as they have plenty of grass (hay) and plants to eat, and ground in which they can dig a warm, safe home, wild rabbits can live and breed almost anywhere.

It is important to realise that rabbits are prey animals and are a major source of food for many meat-eating animals (predators).

Pictured:
The European rabbit,
Oryctolagus cuniculus,
the ancestor and wild
cousin of all our pet
rabbits.

They are hunted by animals on the ground – some even enter their underground homes – and from birds in the air. This means that all rabbits are continuously on the lookout for danger. There is safety in numbers and, if there are a lot of rabbits living together, they can warn each other of danger, making themselves harder to catch. If a predator approaches, the alarm signal is given by a rabbit thumping the ground with its hind legs, and all the rabbits run to the safety of their underground home.

Wild rabbits live in family groups in a rambling underground home called a warren. There are many entrances and exits, sleeping areas and even nursery burrows for litters of baby rabbits (kits). Rabbits are active animals and wild rabbits will travel the length of 30 tennis courts every day as they eat grass and socialise.

This natural behaviour needs to be considered when providing accommodation for dwarf rabbits. They need shelter, and to be able to run, jump, dig and forage every day.

If a female rabbit (doe) is expecting young, she will make a nest using hair from her underbelly. The babies are born without fur, their eyes are closed and they cannot hear. But they develop very quickly. Within two months they no longer need to be cared for by their mother, and within four months the young rabbits are ready to breed.

Wild rabbits have their babies in the spring and summer, and they have several litters a year. On average, there are five kits in a litter, so a single female may have 30 babies in a year, and may even be a grandmother by autumn. So, the numbers of rabbits can grow at a great rate.

Rabbits are social animals and research has shown that they need to have a companion, ideally another rabbit of a similar size and age, if they are not to suffer.

Spot the difference

Hares and rabbits both belong to the Lagomorph family, and look very alike. They eat the same food, and they are both hunted by larger predators. But the hare and the rabbit have found different ways to survive in the wild.

The rabbit escapes its enemies by fleeing underground. The hare lives above ground and relies on its speed. Hares have longer legs than rabbits, which means they can run faster. If a hare is being chased it can reach a speed of 45 miles per hour (72 kilometers per hour) to out-run its enemy.

Baby hares (leverets) are born fully furred with eyes open, ready to run. Baby rabbits are born blind and without fur. To find out more about wild rabbits, and hares, see the suggested further reading at the end of this book.

The human link

For at least two thousand years humans have kept wild rabbits to provide a source of meat and fur. This began with the Romans, who kept wild rabbits in walled enclosures, called Leporaria. The rabbits were left to themselves in terms of breeding.

Following the Roman example, the Normans also kept rabbits, and when they conquered Britain in 1066, they brought rabbits with them. The Normans constructed special rabbit gardens, called warrens, a name that can be found in place names all over Britain, such as Warren Street in London.

The rabbits were confined in a field, where they dug a warren. The field was surrounded by a deep ditch and a high bank to stop rabbits escaping, but they found it easy to dig their way out, and in no time they had spread far and wide.

When the first European settlers were making their homes in the United States and in Australia, the rabbit went along too. Rabbits have been so successful in the wild that they now live in every continent on earth, except Antarctica.

But wild rabbits feast on crops of wheat and vegetables, as well as grass, making them the scourge of farmers. Three rabbits can eat as much grass in a day as one sheep, so a large number of rabbits can do terrible damage to a farm, and they are perceived as are a major menace to agriculture. In many countries, there are continuing attempts to control the numbers of wild rabbits.

Development of the dwarf rabbit breeds

By the 1800s, many people kept rabbits as a source of meat for the table and from this grew the fashion for keeping and breeding the prettier ones. So, by the mid-19th century, people had also started keeping rabbits for showing and as pets.

From the 1850s rabbits were bred for different colours, shapes and coat texture. There were spotted ones, such as the English, giants like the Beveren, and ones with floppy ears – known as Lops – such as the English Lop. However, it was not until the late nineteenth century that very small rabbits were deliberately bred.

The first dwarf rabbit was the tiny white Polish, known as the Britannia Petite in the USA. It was originally developed in Britain in the 1880s and weighs between 1.5- 2.5 lb (700 g - 1.1 kg) when adult.

Around 20 years later, Dutch enthusiasts decided to try and develop an equally tiny rabbit, but with a greater variation of coat colours. They crossed Polish rabbits with small wild rabbits and the result of their breeding experiments was the breed known as the Netherland Dwarf. The Netherland Dwarf weighs 2- 3 lb (900 g – 1.4 kg), has a rounded head and body, with disproportionately large eyes and miniature ears.

The Netherland Dwarf was recognised by the rabbit show world as a breed in its own right in 1940, and arrived in the UK in 1948. It did not become part of the American rabbit show scene until the 1960s.

Dwarf rabbit breeds today

At the time of writing several more dwarf breeds have been developed, all of which weigh less than 5 lb (2.3 kg). They vary in coat colour and texture. Some have lop ears and others erect ears.

In this group are breeds such as the Dwarf Lop, the Himalayan, the Miniature Rex, the Dwarf Angora, and its American counterpart, the rather endearingly named, Jersey Wooly. A recent addition to the list is the descriptively named Lionhead, which has a mane of fur around its head. The Lionhead was first recognised as a breed in the UK in 1995 and in the USA a few years later. Rabbit breed standards are set in the UK by the British Rabbit Council and in the USA by the American Rabbit Breeders Association.

Pictured:
A bright and alert
Dwarf rabbit.

A common characteristic of the dwarf rabbit breeds, apart from their tiny size, is their body shape and the disproportionate ratios of head to eye size and ear length. Some have more flattened faces than larger rabbit breeds. This shape is reminiscent of baby wild rabbits when they are about four weeks old. They look as if they still have to grow up into a 'proper' rabbit shape. It is this baby appearance that many find so appealing.

However, when animals are bred to be very different from the original wild ancestral type, health problems can occur. The wild type shape has been honed by evolution over many centuries to be fit for purpose – in this case, fit for being a rabbit. When humans develop animals that are radically different, such as when they are very much larger or smaller than the wild type, there are genetic and physical changes that accompany the inbreeding that has to take place in order to produce such animals. These can have severely detrimental effects on the health, and behaviour, of the offspring. For dwarf rabbits, these include dental and digestion problems. These will be explained in more detail in the section on health later in this book.

Pictured:
Fresh grasses, herbs and leaves are good for rabbits – but do check the plant is not poisonous.

The dwarf rabbit's world

This section describes how rabbits experience the world. For dwarf rabbits there are some aspects which are different from those rabbit breeds that more closely resemble the wild rabbit shape and size. These differences are noted below.

Nose

The constantly twitching nose shows how important the rabbit's sense of smell is. The rabbit relies on smell to find the best food, to avoid poisonous plants, and to detect the scent of a nearby predator.

Whiskers

The whiskers are used for touch, to measure the width of tunnels, and to help the rabbit find its way in the dark.

Mouth

The rabbit has a large tongue and a sensitive upper lip, which it uses to test if items can be eaten. In the dwarf breeds the mouth is small, and this has implications for what they can eat – for example, they cannot all eat large items of dry food.

Teeth

The rabbit's 28 teeth grow all the time – up to 12.5 cm (5 inches) in a year in large breeds. This is why a constant supply of good quality hay is essential to prevent dental problems, in particular overgrown and mis-shaped (mal-occluded) teeth (see Health section, page 116). Rabbit teeth are specially designed to slice and grind grass and hay – the rabbit's natural food.

Dwarf rabbits are susceptible to dental problems because of the small size of their mouth, and the relatively large size of their teeth.

Eyes

Wild rabbits have an enormous field of vision. This is also true for many domestic breeds where the head is still 'wild rabbit shaped', such as the mini-Rex. They can see behind them, to the sides and above their head, but not right in front of their nose, so approach them from the side so as to not startle them. They have excellent distance vision for movement, to help them detect predators, but they are colour blind.

However, some breeds do not have such a wide field of vision due to the flattened shape of their heads. Breeds such as the Lionhead, which has a large mane, have further restrictions on their ability to see above and behind them. This means it is advisable to talk gently to your rabbits when you approach them so they are not startled.

Ears

Wild rabbits and many breeds of domestic rabbits have upright ears. Each ear can act on its own and be swivelled around so that the rabbit can tune into sound coming from any direction.

The ears on lop-eared breeds, of all sizes, flop down alongside the head, and these rabbits may not hear quite as well and are certainly more prone to developing ear problems.

Some Dwarf rabbit breeds with upright ears, such as the Netherland Dwarf, may also have issues. Their ears are very tiny and less mobile than those of larger breeds. It is likely that they cannot hear as well, and thus may be easily startled.

Front legs

They are strong and short, and are used for digging and balance.

Hind legs

The hind legs are longer than the front legs and are more powerful. They are used for kicking away earth when a rabbit is digging and for kicking out in defence. Rabbits also thump the ground with these legs to warn each other of danger.

Feet

The soles of the feet have a covering of fur which provides a firm grip on most surfaces, but not slippery ones such as polished wooden or laminate floors. If a rabbit, or another animal such as a dog, moves fast on such floors it can slip, skid and injure itself. Typical injuries are in the hips and lower back, which can lead to problems such as arthritis in later life. Breeds like the Mini Rex have little fur on their feet and thus are prone to getting sores.

Movement

The longer hind legs give rabbits their hopping gait, and enable them to move very fast, leaping and twisting to avoid predators. When investigating a new area, rabbits will move quite slowly and timidly using a slow, awkward-looking walking movement.

Tail

This is known as the 'scut'. It is short and upturned, usually showing pale hair on the underside. Bucks (males) carry their tails high when defending their territory or courting does (females). Both bucks and does lift their tails high to show the pale underside when they are running away from something frightening.

Body

The body of a dwarf rabbit is generally a rounded, compact shape and very light.

Coat

The coat may be short or long. It may feel like velvet or satin.

Effects on behaviour of a dwarf

As we have seen some dwarf rabbits breeds are hampered by their shape in being able to detect objects or sounds in the environment.

This can mean that they seem more skittish, or highly strung. It is important to remember they are still prey animals and act in a similar way to their wild ancestors. They are very alert to any new or sudden sound, smell or sight, as all of these may be dangerous. Thus, it is likely that the highly-strung nature of dwarf rabbits is derived from wild rabbits being easily frightened, exacerbated by their compromised sensory abilities. There may also be a more direct genetic link in making them more predisposed to being frightened.

Colours & markings

Dwarf rabbits come in a range of colours and markings. Many are self-explanatory, but the list below will help you understand a selection of the more common terms:

Agouti

Similar to the colour of a wild rabbit, the coat has more than one colour on each strand – usually grey and brown. Blue: an even blue grey. Broken marked: like 'Butterfly' (below), but more varied markings on predominantly white fur.

Butterfly

White with a butterfly-shaped colour marking on the nose. Coloured ears and patches around the eyes, a large coloured patch on the back and variable amounts of spotting.

Chocolate

Deep brown with light grey undercoat.

Chinchilla

Almost silver, like a chinchilla.

Fawn

Deep golden colour on back, flanks and chest. White eye circles, inner ear, chin, belly and tail.

Lilac

Pink/dove grey.

Otter

Black, blue, chocolate or lilac coloured with a creamy white belly that blends to tan coloured edges.

Sealpoint/ Siamese

Like Siamese cats, a beige-grey body colour with a darker coloured face, ears, paws and tail.

Tortoiseshell/ Sooty fawn

Also called 'Madagascar'. Orangey-brown top coat with a blue undercoat. Sides, face, ears, legs, feet and tail are dark grey.

Steel

Similar to chinchilla, but darker.

Brindle pattern

Mix of two colours, one light and one dark, consistently across the body.

Broken pattern

Bi-colour or Tri-colour.

Marked pattern

Usually white with one other coloured pattern all over.

Self pattern

One solid colour.

Tan pattern

Solid colour head, back, sides, outer ear, front foreleg, back legs and top of tail. Lighter eye circles, chest and underside.

Ticked pattern

Majority base colour with contrasting solid or tipped guard hairs.

Dwarf rabbit breeds

There are several breeds of dwarf rabbits, and a range of colours. They vary in size from just 1.5 to 5 lb (700 g – 2.3 kg) when full grown.

Please note that the dwarf rabbits shown in the breed section are not perfect 'breed standard' examples. They are pet dwarf rabbits, more like those available from pet stores. For accurate breed standards, visit the websites of The British Rabbit Council or American Rabbit Breeders Association. The breeds are arranged according to size.

Polish (Britannia Petite)

Size: 1.5– 2.5 lb (0.7– 1.1 kg)

Colour: Usually white with red or blue eyes. Other colours available.

Ears: Erect

The tiny Polish is the oldest of the dwarf breeds and is less rounded in shape than others, with small erect ears.

Netherland Dwarf

Size: 1.5– 2 lb (0.7– 1.1 kg)
Colour: Various colours
Ears: Erect

The Netherland Dwarf is similar in size to the Polish,
but has a more rounded body and head,
again with small erect ears.

The Lionhead

Size: 3– 3.8 lb (1.36– 1.7 kg)
Colour: Various colours and patterns
Ears: Erect

The Lionhead gets its name from its lion-like mane, which forms a full circle around the head and falls into a fringe between the upright ears. However, not all Lionheads keep a full mane as they grow older.

The Lionhead needs more frequent grooming than other breeds to keep the mane free from dirt and tangles. When young they need more brushing until they get their adult coat, which is less woolly.

Miniature Lion Lop

Size: 3.4– 3.8 lb (1.5– 1.7 kg)
Colour: Various colours and patterns
Ears: Drooping

This breed is similar to the
Lionhead except it has wide,
long, drooping ears.

Miniature Lop

Size: 3.4– 3.8 lb (1.5– 1.7 kg)
Colour: Various colours and patterns.
Ears: Drooping

This breed has a shorter coat than
the Lionhead, which therefore
needs less grooming. It is slightly
smaller than the dwarf lop.

Mini or Dwarf Rex

Size: 3.1- 4.8 lb (1.7- 2 kg)
Colour: Wide range of colours &
         patterns.
Ears: Erect

Rex rabbits originated in France in the early 1900s.
The standard coat is very velvety, which was prized by
fur traders in the past. Its texture means that the Rex
needs extra bedding for warmth and comfort. They are
very popular as show rabbits. There are some other
coat types, including the rare Astrex and Opossum.

Size: 4.4 lb (2 kg)

Colour: White with black, chocolate, blue or lilac
points on paws, nose and ears. Pink eyes.

Ears: Erect

The Himalayan is a very old breed and is in fact one
of the original colour variants to be created as a
food stock breed in Asia. This small, slim rabbit has
quite distinctive markings. The breed is classified as
cylindrical, as they have long tube-like bodies (they
are even judged at shows in a stretched out position).
The coat is mainly white, but the short, erect ears,
nose (and face), tail and feet are coloured with black,
blue, chocolate or lilac. They are born white with
markings that develop with age. They have
red/pink eyes.

Notice how their long bodies
differ from the more
rounded rabbit
breeds.

Tan

Size: 4.4 lb (2 kg)

Colour: Black and tan, black, blue, chocolate and tan.

Ears: Erect

The standard colouration of the Tan is similar to that of a Doberman dog, although the two are rarely compared!

The breed dates back to the 1880s. The origin of the first 'Black and Tan' is still something of a mystery, though it is most likely the result of crossing of wild and Dutch rabbits. Various crossings have created other colour combinations since then.

Most commonly found with a black body, with tan underside, eye circles, ears, nose and tail, it has a solid, rounded body.

Dwarf Lop (Holland Lop in USA)

Size: 4.4– 5 lb (2- 2.2 kg)
Colour: Various colours and patterns.
Ears: Drooping

This popular show breed was developed in Holland
in the 1950s from the much larger French Lop – a
breed that weighs over 10 lb (4.5 kg). The dwarf lop
was first recognised as a distinct show breed by the
British Rabbit Council in 1976.

Dutch

Size: 4.4- 5 lb (2- 2.2 kg)

Colour: Black, blue, chocolate, yellow,
tortoiseshell, grey.

Ears: Erect

The Dutch rabbit looks as if it is dressed for a
High Society dinner, in the best of tuxedos! It is
characterised by a bright white inverted 'V'
marking along the bridge of the nose,
a white band around the torso, and white
paws. The rest of the body can be a range
of colours including black, blue, chocolate,
yellow, tortoiseshell and grey and tri-colour.
The coat is quite short and should be glossy.

One dwarf rabbit or two?

Dwarf rabbits are social animals and it is very important that you have two, so that when you are not able to spend time with them they will not be lonely. This need to provide our rabbits with suitable company is recognised in law in the UK Animal Welfare Act (2006) as part of our responsibility for caring for them.

The most successful arrangement is to have a neutered male and neutered female. Dwarf male rabbits can be neutered at around three to four months of age, and females at five to six months. Neutering will mean that you won't have unexpected baby rabbits, which you may not be able to find good homes for.

Wait for me, we rabbits should stay together!

Neutering also helps prevent behaviour problems. These include fighting between rabbits of the same sex, spraying urine (which is part of normal courtship behaviour) and pulling fur. The latter is part of natural nesting behaviour and can be triggered by true or false pregnancy.

Two neutered males, who have known each other since a few weeks old, can also live happily together. However, if not neutered they are likely to fight when adult.

It is not recommended to keep two females. As adults they may fight even if they have been neutered.

If you currently have only one dwarf rabbit, you may wish to consider getting it a companion. However, if it has lived on its own for a long time it may not welcome another rabbit. In that case, you must make sure your rabbit gets plenty of attention from you, every day.

Rabbits & guinea pigs

It is not advised to keep dwarf rabbits and guinea pigs together for several reasons. First, although a single rabbit and guinea pig will provide some sort of company for each other, it will not be as good as having a member of their own kind who 'speaks the same language'.

In addition there are medical reasons why guinea pigs and rabbits may not be the best of cage mates. A rabbit may injure a guinea pig either by kicking it or attempting to mate with it. In addition they have different dietary requirements, as guinea pigs need extra Vitamin C. Finally, guinea pigs are at risk of developing a respiratory disease which is caused by a type of bacteria carried by rabbits and dogs.

You seem nice,
but do you speak
rabbit?

Setting up home

Before you buy your dwarf rabbits, you will need to decide where you are going to keep them, and then buy suitable housing. Most breeds of rabbits, including dwarf rabbits, have furred bottoms to their feet and grow thick winter coats if they live outside. They usually tolerate cooler conditions better than hot ones, and the ideal temperature range is 50- 68°F (10- 20°C).

They can cope with colder conditions, even snow, if their home is not damp or draughty and has plenty of bedding. However, because of their small size, dwarf rabbits lose heat more quickly than larger breeds so you need to ensure that they have suitable accommodation. Where weather is very cold or damp you should seriously consider housing them indoors.

Pictured:
Two examples of hutches. Remember the bigger the better, and rabbits also need a run.

Remember too, that rabbits easily suffer from heatstroke. Accommodation should be well ventilated, but not draughty, and in the shade.

Whether you keep them outside or in your home, the rabbits' accommodation must have both a safe sleeping area (a hutch or cage) and a permanently attached exercise area (run) that they can access when they want to. Ideally, you should also have an additional run that you can move around the garden, or safe areas where they can go free in your home (see further reading).

As an absolute minimum, the hutch/cage should allow each fully-grown rabbit to take three hops and stand up fully on its back legs. It is recommended that the minimum size is 6 feet x 2 feet x 2 feet high (1.8 m x 61 cm x 61 cm) for a dwarf rabbit. Larger breeds require a significantly larger space.

I may be small but I am active and inquisitive.

The great outdoors

Dwarf rabbits can live in an outside hutch-and-run complex all year round, as long as you take steps to make it as comfortable as possible for them, and ensure that temperatures do not get too extreme. The hutch and run must provide shelter from the prevailing wind and direct sunshine. Rabbits need somewhere cool and shady in hot weather as they are susceptible to overheating.

- Both the hutch and run must be made secure to protect the rabbits from larger enemies, such as cats, foxes and birds. Crows and magpies may attack dwarf rabbits.

- The hutch should be raised off the ground to prevent dampness and draughts.

- The hutch should have a separate sleeping compartment, lined with paper and with a cosy bed of hay and straw. The rest of the hutch should also be lined with paper, which helps to absorb the rabbits' urine.

- Other appropriate bedding materials are products made from paper, corn cobs or hardwood. Do not use products made from softwoods as these contain substances that may make your rabbit ill. Wood shavings and sawdust are not recommended as they can cause irritation to the eyes, noses and lungs and dusty bedding can even lead to pneumonia.

- The living quarters should have a fine, wire-mesh front to stop rats or mice getting in.

- A water bottle for small animals and a hay rack should be fitted to the side of the hutch. Water bowls are not always suitable as they can be spilt or fill with bedding.

Rabbits do enjoy drinking from a bowl and it is suggested that a no-spill dog bowl is used in their run, be that indoors or outside. In the winter, a hutch cover should be used. You can buy one ready made, or use some heavy sacking to reduce heat escaping from the roof of the hutch. This will provide extra protection from the cold. The cover can be pulled down over the front of the hutch at night, while still allowing sufficient fresh air. In cold weather, do ensure the rabbits' water has not frozen. Wrapping the bottle will help protect it.

In the summer, if the temperature exceeds 24°C (75°F), all rabbits are susceptible to heatstroke. Ensure they have plenty of water to drink. You can wrap a plastic bottle filled with iced water in a towel, which you can put in the hutch so the rabbits can lie next to it to stay cool. Providing tiling slabs for your rabbits to lay on will also help keep them cool.

Outside run

Rabbits kept in a hutch have limited room to move around, so they need a place where they can exercise. Ideally the run should be permanently attached to the hutch so the rabbits can have free access to it and choose to go out when they want to.

If not, and you have to put your rabbits in the run, you need to provide a shelter. This should be a warm, dry, hay-filled box, raised off the ground, out of the wind and rain. Then your rabbits can go in the run in any weather. They should be given the opportunity to exercise for six to eight hours a day.

The run should be as big as possible, with a shaded area at one end where the rabbits can go if it gets too hot, or if it starts to rain.

Attach a water-bottle to the side of run. A no-spill 'small dog' water bowl can also be provided in the exercise run area, as rabbits of all sizes enjoy lapping water from a bowl.

If the run is on grass, remember to move it regularly so your dwarf rabbits have fresh grass to eat. Make sure you don't put it on grass that has been treated with pesticides.

Pictured:
Runs come in various shapes and sizes and can be freestanding or attached to a hutch.

If the run is on concrete, provide an area filled with sand/soil which will provide a soft resting place. Use sand designed for a child's sand pit.

The run should also contain things for your rabbits to use, and to help them feel safe, such as logs to sit on and use as look-out places, half pipes or other tunnels to run through or hide in. Pet stores stock small tunnels and hide-outs made from edible sticks such as willow, which provide a chewing opportunity too.

House rabbits

Keeping rabbits as house pets started in the USA in the 1980s, and now many owners prefer this way. House rabbits need a hutch or cage to use as a base. Avoid placing it near sunny windows or radiators.

- The indoor hutch/cage should be as big as possible and allow each rabbit to take at least three hops and stand fully erect on its hind legs. You can buy specially-made rabbit cages, or you can adapt a dog crate. It should provide a dark, ventilated, but draught-free resting place.

- The cage needs a shallow tray as a base which can be lined with newspaper, or you can use easy-to-clean carpet tiles.

Pictured:
Enticing your rabbit out of its hutch or cage is preferable to trying to catch it.

- Rabbits will use a litter tray, and this should be placed in one corner of the cage. Line the litter tray with 2.5 cm (1 inch) of dust free cat litter.

  Then add a layer of hay, which will encourage your rabbits to use it.

- You can use washable fleece bedding for a comfortable bed.

- Attach a water bottle to the side of the cage.

There should be an indoor exercise 'run' attached to the hutch/cage so your dwarf rabbits can exercise freely even when you are not there.

Ensure the cage and indoor run are safe from other pets such as cats, dogs and snakes and that the rabbits have places to hide if they feel scared.

Just as with dwarf rabbits kept outdoors, it is important to ensure that your pets can stay cool in summer and that fresh water is always available.

Pictured: Baby rabbits. Note the nest is made from dried grasses and lined with the mother's own soft fur.

Bunny-
proofing
your home

You can use a large playpen so that your rabbits can get exercise outside the cage. Many house rabbit owners 'bunny proof' a room, so the rabbits can hop around in safety. If you let your rabbits go free, watch out for the following hazards:

- Trailing electrical wires.

- Floor-length curtains that are likely to be chewed.

- Houseplants will be seen as a tasty snack and are often poisonous to rabbits.

- Wallpaper shredding is a house rabbit speciality, so confine your rabbit to rooms with painted walls. For more advice about keeping house rabbits see the section on sources of further information.

Pictured:
A Lionhead in its run...
king of the lawn!

Where do I get my rabbits from?

Many of the rabbits in your local pet store will be crossbreeds, which make great pets, and may be larger than pure-bred dwarf rabbits. They will be kept in spacious runs so you can watch them and make your choice.

You could consider giving unwanted rabbits a new home. Some pet stores now have adoption centres and of course there are many associations that are constantly looking to re-home unwanted pets.

Signs of a healthy rabbit

Check that the rabbits you choose are fit and well:

Mouth

Look for signs of dribbling, which could mean the teeth are overgrown.

Eyes

Look for bright, clear eyes, with no discharge.

Ears

Check the inside of the ears to see if they look and smell clean. There should be no sign of damage on the outer ear.

Coat

The coat should be clean and glossy, with no scurf (like dandruff) or bald patches.

Body

The body should be well covered, with no lumps or swellings.

Tail

Check under the tail for any matting or soiling, which could indicate diarrhoea, and is a sign that the rabbit may have teeth or intestine problems, or is too fat.

Breathing

Watching a rabbit's nose twitching will enable you to check its breathing. It should be quiet and regular.

Movement

Look for the typical bunny hop; there should be no sign of lameness.

Bringing home & making friends

Ideally the rabbits' new home should be set up ready for them beforehand. When you first bring your rabbits home you will want to stroke and play with them, but you must be patient.

For the first couple of days, your rabbits need peace and quiet to get used to their new home. Simply provide food and fresh water daily, so your rabbits can get used to you without the stress of being handled. You could whistle gently or call their names before you put the food down. They will soon learn to come when called as they associate your whistle with something pleasant.

If you spend time getting to know your dwarf rabbits, they will become more relaxed and prepared to interact with you. When your rabbits appear to be happy and relaxed, you can start making friends.

To begin with, come close to the hutch or cage, and talk to your rabbits. Do not make any sudden movements, which could alarm them.

Offer treats, so the rabbits come up to you, and get used to your hand.

Now try stroking your rabbits, briefly, just before you give them a treat. Most rabbits love to have their foreheads scratched. Use just one finger to begin with, and gently start to stroke their backs while they are eating.

Only when they are calm and relaxed should you start to use your whole hand to stroke them.

The next stage is to get the rabbit out of the hutch or cage. Be very careful, as dwarf rabbits panic easily and may be injured. Rabbits in general do not like being carried around, and find it very scary. Place one hand underneath the chest, with a finger either side of the front legs, and the other around the hindquarters. Using your hand underneath the rabbit, lift upwards and use your other hand to support the weight. A rabbit should NEVER be picked up by his ears.

As soon as the rabbit is out of the hutch, settle him on the ground. When your rabbit becomes tamer, try holding him on your lap, while you sit on the floor. This process is much easier if the rabbit can access the run from the hutch, as it means you will not be scaring him as you try to catch and carry him from the hutch to the run. Sitting on the floor with your rabbit means he is less likely to be injured if he should wriggle or jump away. Never pass a rabbit to a child while you are standing, as the height and motion of being passed from one person to another can be very frightening and cause him to panic. It would be a bit like you being passed from the top of one skyscraper to another!!

A frightened rabbit can move very fast and may kick or bite. Potentially this could lead to him being dropped or squeezed too hard, as you or the child try to hold him still. Squeezing can cause damage to the internal organs and even break fragile rib bones.

Dwarf rabbits will prefer being gently stroked while sitting on your lap, or next to you rather than being picked up and held.

Never turn your rabbit on its back and stroke his tummy. He will lie very still, because he is scared. He may be trying to pretend to be dead and thus of no interest to a predator. He will remain like this until he thinks the scary thing has gone away, such as when you relax or move your hands away. This is a common behaviour in many small animals. Do not be fooled into thinking that your dwarf rabbit is relaxed or in a trance. Research has shown that they are very alert and stressed. When he thinks it is safe to do so he will suddenly kick out to 'escape' and either you or your rabbit may get injured.

Pictured:
Dwarf rabbits need to be held gently and securely to prevent injury. Do always supervise young children.

Other pets

If you have other pets, such as a dog, cat or ferret, you will need to be very careful, especially if you are keeping house rabbits or allow your rabbits free access to areas where other pets are around.

To start with, the dog should meet the rabbits when they are safely in their hutch or cage. The rabbits will feel frightened, so keep the dog at a distance. Reward the dog with a tasty treat if he remains calm and well behaved. Repeat this exercise many times until the dog loses interest in the rabbits. But remember, you should never allow other pets near the rabbits without supervision. Dogs, cats and ferrets are meat-eaters and rabbit is one of their natural foods.

Rabbits can make friends with other pets in the home; but do be vigilant, especially with dwarf and mini rabbits as they are too small to really defend themselves. Rabbits are prey animals, cats and dogs are predators.

Playtime

Dwarf rabbits kept in the house or outside should be allowed to behave naturally. Rabbits are social and inquisitive creatures and, in the wild, would dig burrows, socialise and forage for food. Rabbits must eat plenty of grass or hay to keep their teeth and digestive system in good order.

All rabbits should be given appropriate toys to play with and lots of hay.

Once you have made friends there are many things that you and your dwarf rabbits can do together. You may even wish to teach them tricks.

This can be a great way of bonding with your rabbits and is lots of fun (see Orr and Lewin in further reading). They can even be taught to jump and follow a rabbit agility course!!

You can help your rabbits to live a full life by doing the following:

- Give your rabbits plenty of hay every day.

- Give them toys. Those made of natural, untreated wood, such as willow, are ideal. Do not give hard, plastic toys. They can cause teeth problems and if a rabbit swallows a fragment it may become extremely ill.

- Make a dig box, which is a cardboard box filled with hay and /or children's sandpit sand. You can scatter in some fresh herbs, or pelleted rabbit food. This gives your rabbits the chance to dig among the hay, and chew up the cardboard box – lots of fun for a rabbit! A similar idea is to stuff the cardboard centres of toilet rolls with hay.

- Fill small dog activity balls with the rabbits' daily ration of pelleted food. Your rabbits will learn to roll the ball along to release the treats. Puzzle feeders designed for rabbits are also available and can provide a lot of fun for both of you.

Rabbit behaviour

One of the most rewarding things about owning a pet is learning to understand what it is thinking or feeling. It will also mean that you will detect if your dwarf rabbit is not feeling well and may need to visit your vet.

If you have two or more dwarf rabbits, you will witness natural behaviour as they interact with each other. But you can also learn a lot about a single rabbit by listening to the sounds he makes, and observing his body postures.

Relaxed & happy rabbits

Lying stretched out

A relaxed, contented rabbit may lie on his side or tummy.

People greeting

A rabbit may 'greet' its owner by stretching his head towards you and flattening its ears. This is how he would greet another rabbit.

Sitting/ lying in contact with another

Rabbits are social animals and like to be near each other. You may even see them gently grooming each other.

Binky

Used in play, this is when a rabbit jumps into the air, twisting its head and body in opposite directions.

However, it is also used when rabbits are very frightened and running away from a predator. The movement is intended to confuse the predator and help the rabbit escape to safety. If a rabbit is in a panic he will run all over the place and can easily injure himself. This is why it is important to have your rabbits on the ground when you are playing with them.

Lookout position

The rabbit is on his hind legs, with all senses on the alert, looking out for danger or to see where you are with his dinner!

Chin rubbing

Behaviour mostly seen in bucks. The rabbit is using scent glands under his chin to mark his territory/ property and members of his group. He will do this on objects, on other dwarf rabbits and on you!

Urine spraying

Male rabbits, particularly those that have not been neutered, will sometimes spray urine. This is part of rabbit courtship, and is also used to tell another male that he is in someone else's territory.

Tail bolt upright

A doe will do this when she is ready for mating.

Frightened rabbits

Crouching down

When a rabbit crouches, with ears flat and eyes bulging, he is telling you he is very frightened.

Tail held out, ears flat

An angry or frightened rabbit. Lop-eared rabbits are unable to move their ears much so you will need to know your rabbit well to read its mood. Likewise, dwarf rabbits with small ears, such as Netherland Dwarfs, also have less mobility in their ears than rabbits with larger, erect ears.

Spitting

A sign of aggression, from a frightened or angry rabbit.

Frightened? Not me...
Actually I am washing
my whiskers!

Thumping the ground with hindlegs

This is an alarm signal, used to warn other rabbits of danger.

Listen to your rabbit

Dwarf rabbits often grind their teeth. A rapid, gentle grinding sound means your rabbit is content; a slow, harsh, grinding sound means he is in pain.

Cooing/ purring

A doe may coo to her young, or rabbits may coo to each other if they are relaxed and secure. They may even do so when you are gently stroking them.

Growling

A noise made by a frightened or angry rabbit.

Screaming

Hopefully you will never hear this. It is a shriek made by an extremely terrified rabbit.

Food, glorious food

A well-balanced diet will keep your dwarf rabbits healthy, and will help to ensure a long life.

In the wild, rabbits eat grass and plants. It is essential that rabbits eat a lot of food which contains high fibre, such as hay and fresh greens. This stops their teeth growing too long, and ensures their digestion and guts remain healthy. If not they can quickly suffer from gut stasis, where the gut no longer works, leading to death. Lack of hay also leads to serious and painful dental problems. Both teeth and digestive problems are common in dwarf rabbits. They are a cause of expensive vet bills, and sadly, often a shortened life.

It is very important not to over-feed, particularly if you have house rabbits. Rabbits living in a hutch outside need more food to give them the energy to stay warm. House rabbits do not need to do this, and can easily become overweight and obese (see Rabbit Health).

Pictured:
Variety is the spice of life, but treats such as carrots should be given sparingly.

Hay

Rabbits need a high level of fibre in their diet, and this is supplied by eating hay or grass. Dried grass is available, but hay is usually easier to obtain. Make sure you buy good-quality hay that smells sweet. Meadow or timothy hay is ideal. Do not feed hay that is dusty or mouldy.

Hay should be available to your rabbits at all times, and should form the main part (80%) of their diet.

Vegetables

Rabbits love fresh vegetables. The best plan is to introduce one vegetable at a time so that your rabbits get used to it.

Dwarf rabbit favourites include clover, sorrel, dandelion leaves, spinach, watercress and herbs, including basil, mint, parsley and coriander. They also enjoy celery, sweetcorn and broccoli tops. Carrots are full of sugar and should only be given sparingly as a treat, sliced into thin strips.

Some leafy vegetables should be offered with caution as they can cause digestive problems such as bloat or diarrhoea. By introducing them in small amounts, one at a time, you will isolate any potentially problematic vegetables.

These include cabbage (which can cause bloat in young rabbits), spring greens and cauliflower (feed the leaf only, not the head). Other leafy greens can be offered in small quantities. If larger amounts are given, especially if the rabbit is not used to fresh greens, these can trigger serious digestive upsets and diarrhoea. Avoid salad vegetables such as tomatoes, lettuce and cucumber which, although much enjoyed, have no beneficial properties and can cause diarrhoea.

When giving any fresh food to your pet it is important to make sure it is rinsed well under cold water to clean away any dirt or insects. You should never feed any fruit or vegetable that is over or under-ripe or that is wilting, as this is not healthy for your rabbits. A good rule of thumb to follow is: would you eat it? If not, then do not feed it to your pet.

Never collect fresh plants from the side of the road or from areas that have been, or are likely to have been, sprayed with pesticides as this will harm your rabbits. Instead try to grow your own fresh herbs and vegetables for your pets. Not only will they taste fresh and crisp but it will also be great fun for your children or yourself to grow the treats.

Never give your rabbits grass cuttings from the lawn mower, as these may be contaminated with exhaust fumes and metal particles.

Complementary diets, supplementary feeding

There are a number of commercial diets that are specially made for rabbits, which contain the nutrients needed to keep your rabbit healthy.

Because rabbits are naturally 'fussy' eaters, known as selective feeders, pelleted diets are better than mixes, which resemble human muesli breakfast cereals. However, whichever type you choose, these should not form the bulk of your rabbits' diet. Overfeeding of such diets can lead to problems with your rabbits' teeth and intestines, obesity, flystrike and boredom. As a rough guide, 0.8 oz (25 g) of a complete pelleted diet per

2.2 lb (1 kilo) of bodyweight is appropriate. Even the larger dwarf breeds (such as the Dutch or Lionhead) only need 1.5 oz (50 g) of pelleted food daily. You will need to weigh it out.

Pictured:
A 'muesli' style food.

How much?

Rabbits are grazers, so they eat throughout the day and night. Hay should always be available for them. Vegetables and their ration of commercial diet can be given once a day or split over two feeding times.

As a rough guide 70% of your rabbits' diet should be hay, 20% fresh vegetables and only 10% pellet or muesli-type rabbit food.

Rabbit care

Looking after dwarf rabbits means keeping their home clean and a close watch for health problems.

Dwarf rabbits can live 10 years, but sadly many only live for less than half that time. This can be because owners do not fully understand the needs of their pets and may not provide a suitable diet and adequate accommodation.

Handling your pet every day and performing regular health checks will help you pick up on the early signs of ill health, and take action quickly to treat ailments before they become too serious. This is best done while handling your pet in the normal way. You should do any examinations as part of your grooming and regular play.

Weigh your rabbits on a regular basis and remember to keep a record of their weight. Once they are full grown it should remain constant. Put your rabbit in a small box on the scales and note the weight. Then weigh the box without the rabbit. The difference between the two is your rabbit's weight.

Even a few ounces up or down in the weight of a dwarf rabbit can indicate that all is not well.

You should know how your pet behaves while healthy. A change in normal patterns of behaviour can also indicate ill health– for example, being less active, being wobbly, altering eating or drinking habits, hiding more or becoming aggressive.

As a guide, signs of a poorly rabbit can include a greasy coat, sitting still with a hunched body, faded, dull or bulging eyes and loose stools. They may press their stomach hard against the floor or roll to the side, or you may see panting while your rabbit is looking distressed. It is important that you contact your vet as soon as possible if you have see any of these signs as their condition can become very serious, even fatal, within just a few hours.

Whether you are going to the vet for a check up or because your dwarf rabbit is ill, take him in a secure box, such as a cat-carrier.

Pictured:
When holding your
rabbit, support its
bottom and make sure
it cannot jump out of
your hands.

IDaily tasks

- Remove all uneaten food and wash the bowls. If you frequently find uneaten food in the bowls, it may mean you are feeding too much, so give less next time. But do check that your rabbit is eating and is not unwell.

- Refill the water bottle/ bowl with fresh water. Check that your rabbit is drinking from the bottle/ bowl. If not it may be that it is not well.

- Refill the hayrack with fresh hay.

- Remove wet bedding and droppings (this is much easier if your rabbits use a litter tray).

- Give your rabbits access to the exercise run for several hours a day. If your rabbit is less active than normal it may not be well.

- Check your rabbit's bottom to ensure it is clean. If not it may be at risk of flystrike, have a digestive upset, or be overweight. In warm weather this should be done twice daily as flystrike can occur very quickly and is fatal if not treated promptly (see Rabbit Care section).

Pictured:
Not a safe way to hold
a rabbit... it can easily
leap off and injure itself!

Weekly tasks

- Confine your rabbits to the exercise area so you can clean the cage or hutch thoroughly.

- Remove all bedding and clean out the cage or hutch with an 'animal-friendly' disinfectant, or a 50:50 solution of white wine vinegar and water.

- If your rabbits use a litter tray, remove all litter, clean the tray, and replace with clean litter.

- Clean the water bottle.

- Replace all bedding material.

- Check your rabbits' teeth, and run your fingers gently along the jaw lines to check for any bumps.

- Check your rabbits' nails.

- Check inside the ears to ensure that they are clean, then sniff for any unusual or pungent odour, which could indicate infection or other problems, Do not try and clean the ears with a cotton bud! Dirty ears need treating by a vet.

- Check the underside of your rabbits' feet for any sores or bald patches.

- Groom your rabbits and check for mites or any other problems.

- Weigh your rabbits to check they are not losing or gaining weight.

Pictured:
A temporary holding place for your rabbit while you clean his home.

Grooming

The amount of grooming each rabbit needs depends on coat length.
All rabbits need brushing weekly, even short-haired ones. However, long haired dwarf rabbits, such as Lionheads and Angoras, will need to be groomed every couple of days to prevent mats and tangles. Grooming helps keep the coat and skin healthy. It also enables you to check for any problems.

A soft human brush or soft brush for small dogs makes an ideal brush for your rabbit. You may need a comb, with rounded teeth, for rabbits with a dense coat, like the Rex. If your rabbit has long hair, ensure you hold the hair below the knot and gently tug with small flicks of the brush. Do not tug or pull too hard or you may pull the hair out from the skin or even tear the skin. If the knot or tangle is not being moved easily, cut it away with a pair of curved surgical scissors.

Start grooming from an early age, perhaps when the rabbit is enjoying some tasty vegetables, so that it learns to relax and enjoy the attention.

Nails

In the wild, a rabbit would keep its nails in trim by digging. A pet rabbit's nails may grow too long, which will make moving very uncomfortable as they can curve over and dig into the feet. Placing some rougher surfaces in your dwarf rabbits' home can help keep their nails in good condition. A simple way is to put a few concrete paving stones or a brick platform that they can walk on. Putting their vegetables on this means they will have to get on to, and walk on, the rough surface, which will help wear the nails.

Nails can be clipped with special nail-clippers, similar to those used for dogs, but you will need to ask a vet or an experienced rabbit-keeper to do this for you, or show you how to do it. You must be careful not to cut an adjacent toe or cut the nail too short to the quick or nail-bed. This is pink coloured as it contains blood vessels and nerves. While easy to see on light coloured nails, if your rabbit has dark nails it can be difficult to judge where the quick is. In that case, trim the nails to the same length as any white ones or just remove the tip. The small size of dwarf rabbits makes this quite a skilled job.

Cutting the nail-bed is very painful and will probably bleed. If it happens, apply some pressure for a 2– 5 minutes until the bleeding stops. Alternatively, dip the toe into some wound powder made specifically for small animals or put a Vaseline or cornflour on the end of the wounded nail to seal it.

Ears

Rabbits can get ear infections, particularly if they have lop ears. Do not try to clean the ears with a cotton bud. Dirty ears need treating by a vet.

Teeth

Keep a very close check on your rabbits' teeth to make sure they do not grow too long. If your rabbits are drooling, have weepy eyes or have difficulty eating (this is one reason to check weight weekly), the teeth may need to be filed down or even removed. This is a job for the vet. Be warned, overgrown teeth can lead to serious and even fatal problems for rabbits. The chances of your rabbits developing tooth problems are much less if they have lots of hay and vegetables to eat.

Dwarf rabbits are particularly prone to developing serious dental problems because their mouths are very small, yet they still have the same number of teeth as large breeds. Their teeth grow quickly – not only the ones you can see, but also the molars at the back of the mouth. These can grow sharp spurs which can damage your rabbit's tongue and stop him eating and drinking. As these are very difficult to see, it is strongly advised that your dwarf rabbits' teeth are checked by a vet every two months.

Pictured:
A fine set of healthy
front teeth.

Health conditions

Vaccinations

Dwarf rabbits can be vaccinated against two serious infections – Myxomatosis and Viral Haemorrhagic Disease (VHD/ RHVD/ RCD). These diseases are fatal and vaccination offers the best possible chance of immunity. Even rabbits kept indoors are at risk and should be vaccinated.

Myxomatosis vaccination needs to be repeated every 6 months, and VHD once a year. Consult your vet for advice.

The sick bed

It is prudent to have a spare cage available if you have a sick or injured rabbit. Keep them in sight of your other dwarf rabbits to prevent stress unless you are told otherwise by your vet.

Illness & injuries

When accidents, injuries or illness occur you should contact your vet as soon as possible, but in the first instance you are responsible for providing the best care you can.

Pictured:
Remember your rabbit
is small and sensitive,
be very gentle when
interacting with him.

Mishaps

Because rabbits are so easily frightened they may be dropped or hurt when trying to run away from something that has scared them. They have very fine bones which can easily fracture. If you believe your pet has suffered a broken or fractured bone, phone your vet immediately. Your vet may advise you to bring your rabbit in as soon as possible for stabilisation and pain relief. Take your rabbit to the vet in a box lined with some soft bedding, and in the meantime keep him in a darkened and quiet area. He will feel safer and more relaxed in a dark enclosed space, such as a cat carrying box.

Wounds

Injuries to paws and eyes are very common in rabbits, often through hay seed or hay strands becoming lodged in their feet or tear ducts. Bites from cage mates may also occur, especially on the ears or nose.

Such injuries may indicate all is not well between your dwarf rabbits and that they do not have enough space or things to do. You should seek behaviour advice from your vet.

Most minor injuries can be treated at home with a salt wash solution and a cotton pad, but more serious injuries must be looked at and treated by a vet as soon as possible to prevent infection and abscesses, which can be particularly serious in dwarf rabbits. Try to keep the wounded area as clean as possible until you can see a vet. The best way to do this is to prepare a solution of rock salt and warm water. Cover the wound after washing to prevent any further risk of infection entering the wound until you can visit your vet.

Injuries to the eyes can be more serious. A saline (rock salt and water) wash to flush the eye and release any foreign bodies is worthwhile, carefully done using a pipette. You should contact your veterinary surgeon at once if the eye is held closed or appears opaque. The sight in the eye, or the eye itself may be lost if treatment is delayed.

Constipation & diarrhoea

If your rabbit is not eating or drinking, or there is any change in the size or consistency of its droppings, then you must contact a vet. These changes should be taken very seriously as they can have a number of causes and can rapidly become fatal. They can be caused by a poor diet, pain or an illness. It may also mean your rabbit has eaten something poisonous. Rabbits are unable to vomit, so everything they eat has to go through the whole gut, meaning that they can become very ill if they eat the wrong thing. Consult a vet for advice and treatment.

Bloat

Bloat occurs when there is a build up of gas in the stomach and the bowel, typically the caecum. It can be fatal for dwarf rabbits. It can be caused by a wide variety of problems including stress, secondary infections, liver coccidiosis, foreign bodies or a sudden change in diet. The most obvious signs of bloat are a swollen hard stomach, lack of appetite, lethargy and dehydration. Veterinary advice should be sought immediately. A similar condition called mucoid enteropathy is seen in rabbits younger than 12– 16 weeks of age.

Respiratory infections

Rabbits commonly carry bacteria which can cause lung disease, and pneumonia is not uncommon. An upper respiratory tract condition called 'snuffles' is also seen. Rabbits are more prone to respiratory problems if they live in a damp, dirty or poorly ventilated environment or are overcrowded.

If left untreated these infections can lead to pneumonia. Consult your vet for further advice. Note that rabbits with a pale discharge from their eyes frequently have underlying dental disease. If you see such a discharge, contact your vet.

Teeth

Dental disease is common in all rabbits and in dwarf and lop breeds in particular. Dental problems that occur in young rabbits less than four months old are likely to be congenital, that is to say that it is just the way that rabbit is put together. Incisor tooth malocclusions are a typical example. Either the upper or lower incisor teeth fail to meet and wear against their opposite number, allowing them to overgrow. Incisor extraction by your vet may solve this problem. In older rabbits the problem is likely to be acquired dental disease and this is usually linked to poor diet, in particular a lack of hay leading to inadequate wear of the cheek teeth. In the worst cases tooth root abscesses can develop and the condition can become intractable. Long term treatment, with repeated anaesthetics may be required. Even then, secondary abscesses and bone infection may result. Many rabbits with advanced dental disease have to be euthanised.

Ears

It is really important to check your rabbit's ears, especially if they are Lops with drooping ears. Because these are not open to the air but hang close to the rabbit's head, they provide an ideal breeding ground for all sorts of infections.

Head tilt

This is often caused by a middle ear infection called Otitis media. It can progress quite slowly and not be noticed until the rabbit has developed a tilt, holding its head to one side. In severe cases it may start to fall over to one side as its balance is affected. Take your rabbit to the vet to get a diagnosis, in case there is some other cause. There is no cure for Otitis media, but many rabbits with a tilt can cope quite well and continue to enjoy life.

Parasites

Scratching and/ or hair loss is a common symptom of skin complaints often brought about by parasites such as lice, mites, mange and fleas, or by fungal infections such as ringworm. These can occur if your rabbit has been stressed or can be passed on from other animals. Some, like ringworm, can affect people too.

Rabbits are usually free from parasites but should your pet get an infestation, treatment may involve injections or specialised medicated shampoo, mild insecticide powder or small animal spot-on preparation. Do not use treatments designed for dogs and cats as these can be fatal to rabbits. You should seek veterinary advice. The most common parasite is the fur mite Chyletiella. This causes scruffy, flaky patches of dandruff-like skin. Look really closely and you may see the mites move, hence its alternative name of wandering dandruff.

Fly strike

Normally a problem in the warmer months, it is caused by blow flies and house flies laying eggs in faeces-soiled fur around the rabbit's bottom. These hatch within 24 hours and eat their way into the skin around the rabbit's rectum. You should check your pet on a daily basis to ensure their bottoms are free from faeces.

There are treatments which can help prevent flies being around the cage/ hutch, but these are not 100% effective, so you must check your rabbit daily.

If you see fly eggs or maggots you should contact your vet immediately. Delay can result in your rabbit being literally eaten alive by maggots.

Worms

Worms are rare in pet rabbits, although roundworms and tapeworms are occasionally a problem. Symptoms include a distended abdomen, poor coat, a crouching posture and (rarely) worms in the faeces. Occasionally cyst-like intermediate forms of tapeworms may develop in rabbits exposed to grass soiled by unwormed dogs. These form a fluid-filled swelling under the skin or deeper in the body.

Rabbit medicine

Veterinary knowledge of rabbits has increased hugely over the last few years and there is much more that can be done for your pet. However, unlike cat and dog medicine, which all veterinary surgeons know a lot about, rabbits are a specialist subject.

Dwarf rabbits are actually considered an exotic species in terms of veterinary care. It is well worth finding a vet who is interested in rabbits and their treatment, and may even have a qualification in exotic animal medicine.

Know your
pet dwarf
rabbit

Scientific name	Oryctolagus cuniculus
Group order	Lagomorpha
Female breeding period	Induced ovulation
Gestation	30- 33 days from successful mating
Litter size	1- 4 (average)
Birth weight	40 g approx
Birth type	Naked, blind, dependent
Eyes open	10- 12 days approx
Weaning	5- 6 weeks
Breeding age	
Doe	4- 5 months; from 6 months optimum
Buck	3- 4 months

Sources of further information

McBride, E.A. 1988 Rabbits and Hares
London, Whittet Books.

McBride, A. 2000 2nd Edition Why Does My Rabbit....?
London Souvenir Press

Magnus, E. 2002.
How to have a relaxed rabbit
UK, Pet Behaviour Centre.

Moore, L.C. 2005 A House Rabbit Primer
California, Santa Monica Press.

Orr, J and Lewin, T 2005
Getting Started: Clicking With Your Rabbit
Karen Pryor Publications.

Richardson, V 1999 Rabbit Nutrition: an illustrated
guide to plants and vegetables, wild and cultivated
that can be fed to your rabbit. Coney Publications.

Websites

www.rabbitwelfare.co.uk – the Rabbit Welfare Association provides lots of useful information and resources on rabbits, including a list of veterinary surgeons around the UK who have a special interest in treating rabbits.

www.rabbit.org – website of the House Rabbit Society of the USA which also provides lots of useful information and resources.

http://wales.gov.uk/docs/drah publications/091109rabbitsumen.pdf - How to look after your rabbit – following the code. A booklet produced by the Welsh government giving advice on your legal responsibilities to your rabbit under the UK Animal Welfare Act (2006).

http://www.hoppingmad. org – a free online rabbit magazine which provides useful information on keeping rabbits, their health and behaviour issues.

Weights & measures

If you prefer your units in pounds and inches, you can use this conversion chart:

Length in inches	Length in cm	Weight in kg	Weight in lbs
1	2.5	0.5	1.1
2	5.1	0.7	1.5
3	7.6	1	2.2
4	10.2	1.5	3.3
5	12.7	2	4.4
8	20.3	3	6.6
10	25.4	4	8.8
15	38.1	5	11

Measurements rounded to 1 decimal place.